First edition

By Lea Coquille-Chambel

# WHAT IF I MOVED ON ?

2022 EDITION

IN ORDER TO MOVE ON, YOU MUST START BY UNDERSTANDING ALL YOUR CHAPTERS.

SOME BREAK-UPS ARE HARDER TO ACCEPT THAN OTHERS. THE DESIRE TO TALK ABOUT IT, THE FEELING OF BEING MISUNDERSTOOD, OVERWHELMING EMOTIONS THAT PUT YOUR DAILY LIFE ON HOLD.

RID YOURSELF OF THIS ILL FEELING, WRITE IT OUT, PUT YOUR EMOTIONS INTO WORDS.

FIND THE FEELING OF A LIGHT HEART AGAIN.

YOU HAVE THE RIGHT TO BE SAD AND HURT, BUT ACCEPTING THE PAIN IS THE ONLY WAY TO HEAL.

THIS JOURNAL GIVES YOU THE OPPORTUNITY TO CONFIDE WITHOUT ANY JUDGMENT.

ENJOY ANSWERING A SERIES OF QUESTIONS WITHOUT HAVING TO WORRY ABOUT ANYONE ELSE'S EYES.

# What if I moved on ?

In this journal, trace back your relationship, from your beginning together until your end on your own.

Express yourself, let your emotions take over.

No one will read this journal so be honest with your emotions and empty your heart out to begin your light-hearted future.

Don't share any page of this journal and confide yourself.

Am I capable of moving on ?

☐ Yes

☐ No

What if I moved on ?

# Before

## THE RELATIONSHIP

'Forget what happened, but never forget what it taught you.'

# Introducing myself :

## Evaluating myself :

Self-confidence : 10% 20% 30% 40% 50% 60% 70% 80% 90% 100%

Determination : 10% 20% 30% 40% 50% 60% 70% 80% 90% 100%

Patience : 10% 20% 30% 40% 50% 60% 70% 80% 90% 100%

Self-respect : 10% 20% 30% 40% 50% 60% 70% 80% 90% 100%

Honesty : 10% 20% 30% 40% 50% 60% 70% 80% 90% 100%

Humor : 10% 20% 30% 40% 50% 60% 70% 80% 90% 100%

Intelligence : 10% 20% 30% 40% 50% 60% 70% 80% 90% 100%

Tolerance : 10% 20% 30% 40% 50% 60% 70% 80% 90% 100%

Solidarity : 10% 20% 30% 40% 50% 60% 70% 80% 90% 100%

Sociability : 10% 20% 30% 40% 50% 60% 70% 80% 90% 100%

Creativity : 10% 20% 30% 40% 50% 60% 70% 80% 90% 100%

Style : 10% 20% 30% 40% 50% 60% 70% 80% 90% 100%

Health : 10% 20% 30% 40% 50% 60% 70% 80% 90% 100%

Generosity : 10% 20% 30% 40% 50% 60% 70% 80% 90% 100%

Focus : 10% 20% 30% 40% 50% 60% 70% 80% 90% 100%

Talent : 10% 20% 30% 40% 50% 60% 70% 80% 90% 100%

Appearance : 10% 20% 30% 40% 50% 60% 70% 80% 90% 100%

**Before, I didn't want to be in a relationship because :**

**My opinion on love :**

**My past relationships :**

DEAR PAST ME,

Things that make me happy :

Before, those who would flirt with me :

When I wanted to go out, I would call :

If I was to sum up my life before you, I would say :

I ONLY CARED ABOUT :

I WAS SINGLE BECAUSE :

My favorite thing about my body :

My least favorite thing :

People said my personality was :

For me, an ideal relationship was :

Before, when I thought about the future, I imagined :

**MY FRIEND GROUP WAS :**

**MY PROJECTS WERE :**

## How we met, in details :

THE DATE WE MET :

WE STARTED TALKING BECAUSE :

**What I thought about you :**

**What I liked about you :**

WHAT I HATED ABOUT YOU :

A SENTENCE I REMEMBER FROM OUR FIRST DATE :

THAT DAY, WE WERE DRESSED :

Our first date lasted :

Who made the first move :

How long we were talking for :

Here's what I would have liked to tell you when we first met :

# During

## THE RELATIONSHIP

'You deserve more than a chapter. You deserve to be the book they can't help but read.'

## EVALUATING MYSELF :

SELF-CONFIDENCE : 10% 20% 30% 40% 50% 60% 70% 80% 90% 100%

DETERMINATION : 10% 20% 30% 40% 50% 60% 70% 80% 90% 100%

PATIENCE : 10% 20% 30% 40% 50% 60% 70% 80% 90% 100%

SELF-RESPECT : 10% 20% 30% 40% 50% 60% 70% 80% 90% 100%

HONESTY : 10% 20% 30% 40% 50% 60% 70% 80% 90% 100%

HUMOR : 10% 20% 30% 40% 50% 60% 70% 80% 90% 100%

INTELLIGENCE : 10% 20% 30% 40% 50% 60% 70% 80% 90% 100%

TOLERANCE : 10% 20% 30% 40% 50% 60% 70% 80% 90% 100%

SOLIDARITY : 10% 20% 30% 40% 50% 60% 70% 80% 90% 100%

SOCIABILITY: 10% 20% 30% 40% 50% 60% 70% 80% 90% 100%

CREATIVITY : 10% 20% 30% 40% 50% 60% 70% 80% 90% 100%

STYLE : 10% 20% 30% 40% 50% 60% 70% 80% 90% 100%

HEALTH :10% 20% 30% 40% 50% 60% 70% 80% 90% 100%

GENEROSITY :10% 20% 30% 40% 50% 60% 70% 80% 90% 100%

FOCUS :10% 20% 30% 40% 50% 60% 70% 80% 90% 100%

TALENT : 10% 20% 30% 40% 50% 60% 70% 80% 90% 100%

APPEARANCE : 10% 20% 30% 40% 50% 60% 70% 80% 90% 100%

**The date of our first kiss :**

**That day, I felt :**

**Our first activity :**

## OUR TO-DO LIST

- [ ] ..............................
- [ ] ..............................
- [ ] ..............................
- [ ] ..............................
- [ ] ..............................
- [ ] ..............................
- [ ] ..............................
- [ ] ..............................

OUR COMMON SECRET :

THE FIRST I LOVE YOU :

THE TOPIC WE ALWAYS FOUGHT ABOUT :

A TYPICAL WEEKEND TOGETHER :

MY BEST MEMORY OF US TOGETHER :

Our first fight :

I trusted you because :

Your worst flaw :

Your best quality :

## Our favorite :

Restaurant : ................................................................

Trip : ................................................................

Movie : ................................................................

TV show : ................................................................

Song : ................................................................

Thing to do : ................................................................

Position : ................................................................

Meal : ................................................................

Nickname : ................................................................

Animal : ................................................................

Saying : ................................................................

OUR DREAM WAS TO :

OUR HAPPIEST MOMENT :

I FELT LOVED THE DAY :

YOUR MOST BEAUTIFUL GESTURE FOR ME :

## Which one of us ? :

Was the most romantic :

Sent the most texts :

Gave the most compliments :

Was the funniest :

Was the messiest :

Was the most stubborn :

Took up more space in bed :

Spent the most money :

Had the worst temper :

Woke up earlier :

Had more flaws :

## A LETTER FOR US :

## A LETTER FOR US :

In five years, I saw us :

The day I met your parents :

What our friends thought about us :

Our first intimate moment :

The first time I cried for you :

THE THINGS I NEVER TOLD YOU :

# During

## THE BREAK-UP

'Someone who truly loves you will never find a reason to leave. They will look for reasons to stay.'

## EVALUATING MYSELF :

SELF-CONFIDENCE : 10% 20% 30% 40% 50% 60% 70% 80% 90% 100%

DETERMINATION : 10% 20% 30% 40% 50% 60% 70% 80% 90% 100%

PATIENCE : 10% 20% 30% 40% 50% 60% 70% 80% 90% 100%

SELF-RESPECT : 10% 20% 30% 40% 50% 60% 70% 80% 90% 100%

HONESTY : 10% 20% 30% 40% 50% 60% 70% 80% 90% 100%

HUMOR : 10% 20% 30% 40% 50% 60% 70% 80% 90% 100%

INTELLIGENCE : 10% 20% 30% 40% 50% 60% 70% 80% 90% 100%

TOLERANCE : 10% 20% 30% 40% 50% 60% 70% 80% 90% 100%

SOLIDARITY : 10% 20% 30% 40% 50% 60% 70% 80% 90% 100%

SOCIABILITY : 10% 20% 30% 40% 50% 60% 70% 80% 90% 100%

CREATIVITY : 10% 20% 30% 40% 50% 60% 70% 80% 90% 100%

STYLE : 10% 20% 30% 40% 50% 60% 70% 80% 90% 100%

HEALTH : 10% 20% 30% 40% 50% 60% 70% 80% 90% 100%

GENEROSITY : 10% 20% 30% 40% 50% 60% 70% 80% 90% 100%

FOCUS : 10% 20% 30% 40% 50% 60% 70% 80% 90% 100%

TALENT : 10% 20% 30% 40% 50% 60% 70% 80% 90% 100%

APPEARANCE : 10% 20% 30% 40% 50% 60% 70% 80% 90% 100%

## THE REASON WE BROKE UP :

### My emotions that day :

IF I COULD HAVE CHANGED SOMETHING ABOUT OUR RELATIONSHIP :

THE PEOPLE THAT WERE THERE FOR ME :

THEY COMFORTED ME BY SAYING :

## WHAT I WAS REPROACHED FOR :

## MY TOP DEPRESSION SONGS :

1 ........................................

2 ........................................

3 ........................................

4 ........................................

5 ........................................

6 ........................................

7 ........................................

8 ........................................

9 ........................................

10 ........................................

## THE EXACT WORDS OF THE BREAK-UP :

## THE DAY AFTER MY BREAK-UP :

## DRAWING WHAT I'M FEELING :

## What I reproached you for :

## The pros and cons of our break-up :

### Pros :

### Cons :

## WHAT HELPS ME SMILE :

## WHAT MAKES ME THINK ABOUT YOU :

THE DAY AFTER THEIR BREAK-UP :

## THE TOP 10 THINGS THAT HAVE MADE ME HURT :

1 ........................................

2 ........................................

3 ........................................

4 ........................................

5 ........................................

6 ........................................

7 ........................................

8 ........................................

9 ........................................

10 ........................................

I TRIED FIXING THINGS BY :

BUT YOU TOLD ME THAT :

## ALL THE WORDS THAT HURT ME :

BECAUSE OF YOU I :

BUT I OPENED MY EYES ON :

Day-to-day you brought me :

Your last message :

Was I more happy or sad ? :

Do I still want to see you ? :

If you were in front of me I would tell you :

## My apologies :

## THE APOLOGIES I WOULD LIKE TO RECEIVE :

**WAS I RECEIVING ENOUGH ATTENTION ? :**

**WHAT YOU WANTED ME TO CHANGE :**

## WHAT WAS MISSING IN OUR RELATIONSHIP :

Could this relationship have lasted ? :

In bed it was :

## How the break-up affected my lifestyle :

IF YOU MET SOMEONE TOMORROW, I :

WHEN I SEE OUR PICTURES, I :

IS THERE STILL A CHANCE ? :

## If I had to write a letter to myself to open my own eyes, I would say :

**If I had to write a letter to myself to open my eyes, I would say :**

THE PLACES THAT MAKE ME THINK OF YOU :

WE'VE BEEN BROKEN UP SINCE :

AND TODAY I FEEL :

**Since you've been gone, my days look like :**

**Right now, all I want is :**

I WOULD LIKE TO THANK YOU :

## My regrets :

## MY LAST GOODBYE :

## My last goodbye :

# After

## THE BREAK-UP

'If you have been brave enough to say goodbye, life will reward you with a new hello.'

## Evaluating myself :

Self-confidence : 10% 20% 30% 40% 50% 60% 70% 80% 90% 100%

Determination : 10% 20% 30% 40% 50% 60% 70% 80% 90% 100%

Patience : 10% 20% 30% 40% 50% 60% 70% 80% 90% 100%

Self-respect : 10% 20% 30% 40% 50% 60% 70% 80% 90% 100%

Honesty : 10% 20% 30% 40% 50% 60% 70% 80% 90% 100%

Humor : 10% 20% 30% 40% 50% 60% 70% 80% 90% 100%

Intelligence : 10% 20% 30% 40% 50% 60% 70% 80% 90% 100%

Tolerance : 10% 20% 30% 40% 50% 60% 70% 80% 90% 100%

Solidarity : 10% 20% 30% 40% 50% 60% 70% 80% 90% 100%

Sociability : 10% 20% 30% 40% 50% 60% 70% 80% 90% 100%

Creativity : 10% 20% 30% 40% 50% 60% 70% 80% 90% 100%

Style : 10% 20% 30% 40% 50% 60% 70% 80% 90% 100%

Health : 10% 20% 30% 40% 50% 60% 70% 80% 90% 100%

Generosity : 10% 20% 30% 40% 50% 60% 70% 80% 90% 100%

Focus : 10% 20% 30% 40% 50% 60% 70% 80% 90% 100%

Talent : 10% 20% 30% 40% 50% 60% 70% 80% 90% 100%

Appearance : 10% 20% 30% 40% 50% 60% 70% 80% 90% 100%

NUMBER OF DAYS SINCE THE BREAK-UP :

TODAY I FEEL :

A SONG THAT HELPED ME OVERCOME IT ALL :

## MY THOUGHTS TODAY :

My projects :

My friend situation :

In one year I see myself :

## My to-do list

- [ ] ........................................
- [ ] ........................................
- [ ] ........................................
- [ ] ........................................
- [ ] ........................................
- [ ] ........................................
- [ ] ........................................
- [ ] ........................................
- [ ] ........................................
- [ ] ........................................

THE PEOPLE THAT HELPED ME MOVE ON :

AM I ABLE TO MEET SOMEONE NEW ? :

ISN'T IT BETTER THIS WAY ? :

**How I've changed physically since the break-up :**

**Do I still think about this person ? :**

**Was the break-up that hard ? :**

IF I WAS TO WRITE A LETTER TO MYSELF FROM A MONTH AGO :

**What changed in my everyday life :**

**The hobby I have discovered :**

IF I BUMPED INTO YOU TODAY, I WOULD SAY :

THE PHYSICAL FEATURE I HAVE LEARNED TO LOVE AGAIN :

A SKILL I DISCOVERED :

IF I WAS TO REPROACH MYSELF FOR SOMETHING :

A QUOTE THAT DESCRIBES MY STATE :

I GO OUT THESE DAYS :

DO I EAT NORMALLY ? :

DID I MEET SOMEONE NEW ? :

## My day today :

## WHAT I EXPECT FROM THE NEXT PERSON WHO WILL WALK INTO MY LIFE :

## THE MISTAKES I WON'T MAKE AGAIN :

## ALL OF THIS TAUGHT ME :

## AM I HAPPY ? :

## LET'S DRAW

## Expressing myself

## Confiding Myself

## One last word ?

## A SUMMARY OF MY STORY :

TURNING OVER A NEW LEAF SEEMS HARD, YET YOU'VE ALREADY TURNED OVER 100 PAGES SINCE THE BEGINNING OF THIS BOOK.

SO ARE YOU CAPABLE OF MOVING ON ?

☐ YES

☐ NO

'Once it's over, block them and glow up.'

WHAT IF I MOVED ON ?

'If you have to convince someone to stay, it isnt love.'

# What if I moved on ?

Made in the USA
Middletown, DE
22 November 2022